THE CASE FOR FAITH

VISUAL EDITION

LEE STROBEL

creative direction by

MARK ARNOLD

andArnold Books

We want to hear from you. Please send your comments about this book to us in care of zreview@zondervan.com. Thank you.

ZONDERVAN

The Case for Faith Visual Edition

Copyright © 2005 by Lee Strobel

Requests for information should be addressed to:

Zondervan, Grand Rapids, Michigan 49530

ISBN-10: 0-310-25906-1

ISBN-13: 978-0-310-25906-0

Cover and interior design by Mark Arnold/andArnold books.

Printed in China

05 06 07 08 09 10 11 /❖ TPC/ 10 9 8 7 6 5 4 3 2 1

WILLOW
Willow Creek Association

ZONDERVAN™
WWW.ZONDERVAN.COM

The Case for Faith Visual Edition uses excerpts from Lee Strobel's award-winning books *The Case for Christ* and *The Case for Faith*. Most of the text is the product of interviews he conducted with leading experts and scholars. For attribution, and to locate more in-depth discussions of these critical topics in *The Case for Christ* and *The Case for Faith*, please see the reference guide found on page 148 of this edition.

Only in a world where faith
is difficult can faith exist.

God?

God?

Hello?

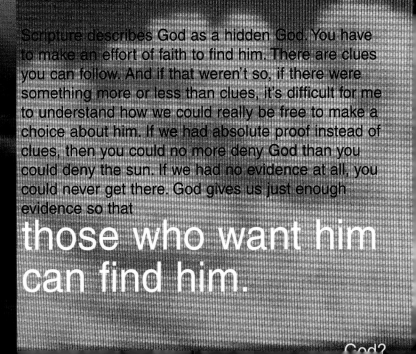

God?

God?

G

God?

Scripture describes God as a hidden God. You have to make an effort of faith to find him. There are clues you can follow. And if that weren't so, if there were something more or less than clues, it's difficult for me to understand how we could really be free to make a choice about him. If we had absolute proof instead of clues, then you could no more deny God than you could deny the sun. If we had no evidence at all, you could never get there. God gives us just enough evidence so that

those who want him can find him.

6

God?

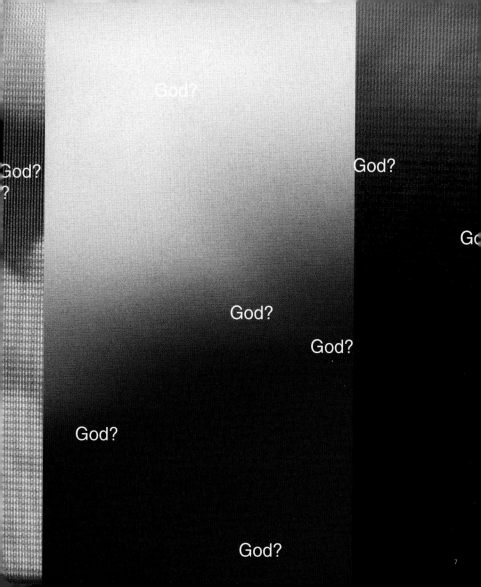

s e

AND YOU WILL FIND.

GOD,

IF IT'S SO IMPORTANT FOR

ME TO BELIEVE IN YOU,

HING REALLY,

He is not far from any one of us. —ACTS 17:27

He is not far from any one of us. —ACTS 17:27

A Sri Lankan man carries the body of his son out from a hospital at the town of Galle, 117 kilometers (70 miles) south of Colombo, Sri Lanka, Monday, Dec. 27, 2004. The death toll from massive tidal waves that struck Sri Lanka's coastline leapt to more than 12,000 as thousands of soldiers and families kept up the search for bodies. (AP Photo/Vincent Thian)

Two-year-old Swedish boy Hannes Bergstroem, right, is reunited with his father Marko Karkkainen in a Phuket hospital, Thailand, Wednesday, Dec. 29, 2004 in this image made from television. Hannes was found alone in the wasteland of a tsunami-hit resort island in Khao Lak, southern Thailand. (AP Photo/APTN)

He is not far from any one of us. —ACTS 17:27

He is not far from any one of us. –ACTS 17:27

"Faith is a rational response to the evidence of God's self-revelation in human history..."—*W. Bingham Hunters*

FULL-

WHAT DO YOU WANT?
The Bible says that if you
seek God with all your
heart, then you will surely
find him. *Surely find him.*
It's the person who wants

Super Savings on Last Minute Cruises!
**7-Night Alaska Cruise
From $399**

to know God that God
reveals himself to. And if a
person doesn't want to
know God—well, God has
created the world and the
human mind in such a way
that he doesn't have to.

Right Now G...
...mos FREE

Best Price

Best Selection

Home Theater
System

SEX?

33 grams
of fat

You're
packing a
suitcase for a place
none of us has been

A place

that has to be believed

to be seen.

—Bono, "Walk On"

at the Big Bang." –Stephen Hawking

Kenny of Oxford University says, "A proponent

came from nothing and by nothing."

look on it as frankly supernatural."

Stephen Hawking calculated that if the rate of the universe's expansion one second after the Big Bang had been smaller by even one part in a hundred thousand million million, the universe would have collapsed into a fireball.

There are about fifty constants and quantities—[ex: the amount of usable energy in the universe, the difference in mass between protons and neutrons and the proportion of matter to antimatter]—their must be balanced to a mathematically infinitesimal degree for any life to be possible.

British physicist P. C. W. Davies has concluded the odds against the initial conditions being suitable for the formation of stars—a necessity for planets and thus life—is a one followed by at least a thousand billion billion zeroes.

P. C. W. Davies also estimated that if the strength of gravity or of the weak force were changed by only one part in a ten followed by a hundred zeroes, life could never have developed.

27

Nobel Prize-winner Sir Francis Crick said, "The origin of life appears to be almost a miracle, so many are the conditions which would have had to be satisfied to get it going."

Even so, scientists have tried to come up with creative theories to try to explain how biopolymers (such as proteins) became assembled with only the right building blocks (amino acids) and only the correct isomers (left-handed amino acids) joined with only the correct peptide bonds in only the correct sequence.

I had been taught in school that if chemicals had an ample amount of time to interact in the "warm little ponds" of early earth, eventually the improbable would become probable and life would emerge.

"Scientists once believed in the idea of random chance plus time yielding life, because they also believed in the steady-state theory of the universe," scientist Walter Bradley said. "This meant the universe was infinitely old, and who knows what could happen if you had an infinite amount of time? But with the discovery of background radiation in 1965, the Big Bang theory came to dominate in cosmology. The bad news for evolution was that this meant the earth was probably less than five billion years old.

"Actually, it's not as long as you think. And not only was the time too short, but the mathematical odds of assembling a living organism are so astronomical that nobody still believes that random chance accounts for the origin of life. Even if you optimized the conditions, it wouldn't work. If you took all the carbon in the universe and put it on the face of the earth, allowed it to chemically react at the most rapid rate possible, and left it for a billion years, the odds of creating just one functional protein molecule would be one chance in 10,000,000,000,000,000,000,000,000,000,000,000,000,000,000,000,000,000,000,000.

"Biochemist Michael Behe has said the probability of linking together just one hundred amino acids to create one protein molecule by chance would be the same as a blindfolded man finding one marked grain of sand somewhere in the vastness of the Sahara Desert—and doing it not just once, but three different times. Sir Frederick Hoyle put it colorfully when he said that this scenario is about as likely as a tornado whirling through a junkyard and accidentally assembling a fully functional Boeing 747.

"In other words, the odds for all practical purposes are zero. That's why even though some people who aren't educated in this field still believe life emerged by chance, scientists simply don't believe it anymore."

SITTING AND BROODING OVER FAITH and doubt will never make a believer out of anybody. Ultimately, you must embark on your experiment of faith by doing what faith would do.

Jesus said that if we continue in his Word—that is, continue doing what Jesus says—then we are truly his disciples. Being a disciple means you're a "following learner." And when you're a following learner, you will know the truth and the truth will set you free.

Knowing the truth doesn't mean filling your head with knowledge; it's experiential knowledge.

You say, "I've heard some things that Jesus taught. They sound like good ideas to me, but I don't know if they're true. For instance, I've heard Jesus say it's more blessed to give than to receive. How can I know if that's true?" Well, a thousand debates won't prove it. But when you become generous, you'll realize this is truth. You might say, "Oh, maybe Jesus accidentally guessed right about that one." Then just keep going. You'll be amazed at how often he "guessed" right!

In Psalm 34:8, King David said, "Taste and see that the Lord is good."

"I.A

M'?

Moses said to God, "If I go to the people of Israel and tell them, 'The God of your fathers has sent me to you,' they won't believe me. They will ask, 'Which God are you talking about? What is his name?' Then what should I tell them?"

God replied, "I AM THE ONE WHO ALWAYS IS. Just tell them, 'I AM has sent me to you.'" —*Exodus 3:13,14*

THE NICENE CREED [AD 325] IS THE MOST WIDELY ACCEPTED AND USED BRIEF STATEMENTS OF THE CHRISTIAN FAITH. IT IS COMMON GROUND TO EASTERN ORTHODOX, ROMAN CATHOLICS, ANGLICANS, LUTHERANS, CALVINISTS, AND MANY OTHER CHRISTIAN GROUPS.

we believe

in one God,
the Father, the Almighty,
maker of heaven and earth,
of all that is, seen and unseen.

we believe in one Lord, Jesus Christ,

the only Son of God,
eternally begotten of the Father,
God from God, Light from Light,
true God from true God,
begotten, not made,
of one Being with the Father.
Through Him all things were made.
For us and for our salvation
He came down from heaven:
by the power of the Holy Spirit

He became incarnate from the Virgin Mary,
and was made man.
For our sake He was crucified under Pontius Pilate;
He suffered death and was buried.
On the third day He rose again
in accordance with the Scriptures;
He ascended into heaven
and is seated at the right hand of the Father.
He will come again in glory to judge the living and the dead,
and His kingdom will have no end.

we believe in the Holy Spirit, the Lord, the giver of life,
who proceeds from the Father and the Son.
With the Father and the Son He is worshiped and glorified.
He has spoken through the Prophets.
We believe in one holy [universal] and apostolic Church.
We acknowledge one baptism for the forgiveness of sins.
We look for the resurrection of the dead,
and the life of the world to come.

Sources from outside the Bible corroborate that many people believed Jesus performed healings and was the Messiah, that he was crucified, and that despite this shameful death, his followers, who believed he was still alive, worshiped him as God. One expert documented thirty-nine ancient sources that corroborate more than one hundred facts concerning Jesus' life, teachings, crucifixion, and resurrection. Seven secular sources and several early Christian creeds concern the deity of Jesus, a doctrine "definitely present in the earliest church."

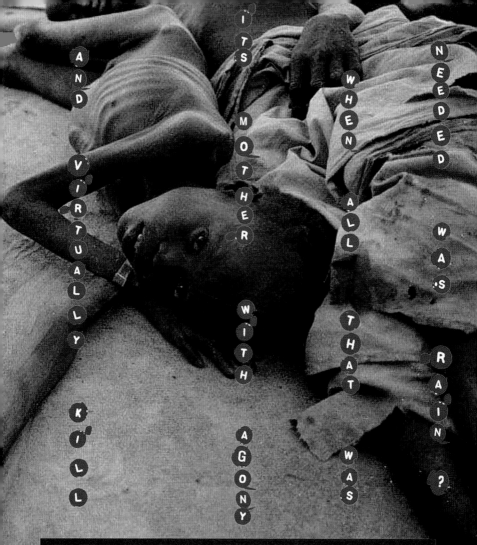

A 10-year-old Sudanese girl lies with her mother and brother inside a compound within famine-torn Bahr el Ghazal province in south Sudan. Starving Sudanese, in conditions so desperate that mothers stare at their skeletal children in horrified disbelief, are dying by the thousands. (AP Photo/Brennan Linsley)

HOW CAN a mere finite human be sure that infinite wisdom would not tolerate certain short-range evils in order for more long-range goods we couldn't foresee? Look at it this way. Would you agree that the difference between us and God is greater than the difference between us and, say, a bear? Yes? Okay, then, imagine a bear in a trap and a hunter who, out of sympathy, wants to liberate him. He tries to win the bear's confidence, but he can't do it so he has to shoot the bear full of drugs. The bear, however, thinks this is an attack and that the hunter is trying to kill him. He

----------//-----------------

doesn't realize that this is being done out of compassion.

Then, in order to get the bear out of the trap, the hunter has to push him further into the trap to release the tension on the spring. If the bear were semiconscious at this point, he would be even more convinced that the hunter was his enemy who was out to cause him suffering and pain. But the bear would be wrong. He reaches this incorrect conclusion because he is not human.

I believe God does the same to us sometimes, and we can't comprehend why he does it any more than the bear can understand the motivations of the hunter. As the bear could have trusted the hunter, so we can trust God.

"Once God chose to create human beings with free will, then it was up to them, rather than God, as to whether there was sin or not. That's what free will means. Built into the situation of God deciding to create human beings is the chance of evil and, consequently, the suffering that results."

"Then God is the creator of evil."

"No, he created the possibility of evil; people actualized that potentiality. The source of evil is not God's power but mankind's freedom. Even an all-powerful God could not have created a world in which people had genuine freedom and yet there was no potentiality for sin. It's a self-contradiction— a meaningless nothing—to have a world where there's real choice while at the same time no possibility of choosing evil. The overwhelming majority of the pain in the world is caused by our choices to kill, to slander, to be selfish, to stray sexually, to break our promises, to be reckless."

"Then why didn't God create a world without human freedom?"

"Because that would have been a world without humans. Would it have been a place without hate? Yes. A place without suffering? Yes. But it also would have been a world without love, which is the highest value in the universe. That highest good never could have been experienced. Real love–our love of God and our love of each other–must involve a choice. But with the granting of that choice comes the possibility that people would choose instead to hate."

Song Name	Time	Ar
☑ I Believe In A Thing Called Love	4:48	B
☑ I Believe In America	4:38	Ja
☑ I Believe In Anarchy	3:34	ca
☑ I Believe In Angels	4:07	Sv
☑ I Believe In Anything	3:36	U:
☑ I Believe In Broadway	4:39	Ti
☑ I Believe In Christ	3:26	O
☑ I Believe In Christmas	3:41	Cl
☑ I Believe In Commercials	7:29	Ri
☑ I Believe In Cowboys	3:53	Gi
☑ I Believe In Dreams	3:26	M
☑ I Believe In Everything A Little	4:42	3
☑ I Believe In Evolution-She Made A Monkey Out of Me	3:37	O
☑ I Believe In Fairytales	3:21	Ri
☑ I Believe In Faith	3:49	U:
☑ I Believe In Fate	4:59	Ri
☑ I Believe In Forever Again	4:59	U:
☑ (Sometimes I Believe In) 4-Leaf Clovers	3:33	ol
☑ I Believe In Getting Paid	4:10	Gi
☑ I Believe In Ghosts	4:26	Cl
☑ I Believe In God	3:43	O
☑ (I Believe In) Good Old Country Music	4:36	Gi
☑ I Believe In Happy Endings	3:41	Ja
☑ I Believe In Heaven	4:36	B
☑ I Believe In Her Love	4:38	Ri
☑ I Believe In J.E.S.U.S.	5:16	Gi
☑ I Believe In Karma	5:49	Ti
☑ I Believe In Love	4:29	M
☑ I Believe In Love Again	4:03	Ri
☑ I Believe In Love Songs	3:52	Ri
☑ I Believe In Magic	5:30	O

Source

Shuffle

Store
...ased Music
...Music
...p Rated
...tly Added
...tly Played
...5 Most Played
...o dismantle

	Title		Time
☑	I Believe In Me		4:01
☑	I Believe In Miracles		4:53
☑	I Believe In Moonlight		4:09
☑	I Believe In Music		3:11
☑	I Believe In My Country		4:54
☑	I Believe In My Song		4:18
☑	I Believe In Nothing		3:16
☑	I Believe In Now		4:48
☑	I Believe In Opa-locka		2:01
☑	I Believe In Partytime		3:59
☑	I Believe In Passion		4:35
☑	I Believe In Peace		1:11
☑	I Believe In People		4:49
☑	I Believe In Rock 'n Roll		5:24
☑	I Believe In Roy Rogers		3:15
☑	I Believe In Romance		5:19
☑	I Believe In Santa Claus		5:11
☑	I Believe In Snuffleupagus		5:08
☑	I Believe In Something		4:03
☑	I Believe In Spirit		3:42
☑	I Believe In Springtime		2:47
☑	I Believe In Steel		5:52
☑	I Believe In Sunshine		7:06
☑	I Believe In Takin' A Chance		4:50
☑	I Believe In The American Way		1:09
☑	I Believe In The Beat		8:45
☑	I Believe In The Blood		4:38
☑	I Believe In The Feelin		3:34
☑	I Believe In The Man in the Sky		4:07
☑	I Believe In The Old Time Way		3:36
☑	I Believe In The Sun		4:39
☑	I Believe In The West Coast		3:26
☑	I Believe In This Love		3:41
☑	I Believe In Tomorrow		7:29
☑	(I Believe In) Travellin' Light		3:53
☑	I Believe In U.F.O.'S		3:26

GOD, DID YOU WANT MY NE
ALZHEIMER'S?

38 46 74 132 134

GHBOR TO GET

The answer to suffering cannot just be an abstract idea, because this isn't an abstract issue; it's a personal issue. It requires a personal response. The answer must be someone, not just something, because the issue involves someone— **"God, where are you?"**

That question almost echoed in his small office. It demanded a response. To philosopher Peter Kreeft, there is one—a very real one. A living One.

"Jesus is there, sitting beside us in the lowest places of our lives," he said. "Are we broken? He was broken, like bread, for us. Are we despised? He was despised and rejected of men. Do we cry out that we can't take any more? He was a man of sorrows and acquainted with grief. Do people betray us? He was sold out himself. Are our tenderest relationships broken? He too loved and was rejected. Do people turn from us? They hid their faces from him as from a leper.

"Does he descend into all of our hells? Yes, he does. From the depths of a Nazi death camp, Corrie ten Boom wrote: 'No matter how deep our darkness, he is deeper still.' He not only rose from the dead, he changed the meaning of death and therefore of all the little deaths—the sufferings that anticipate death and make up parts of it.

"He is gassed in Auschwitz. He is sneered at in Soweto. He is mocked in Northern Ireland. He is enslaved in the Sudan. He's the one we love to hate, yet to us he has chosen to return love. Every tear we shed becomes his tear. He may not wipe them away yet, but he will."

He paused, his confident tone downshifting to tentative. "In the end, God has only given us partial explanations," he said slowly, a shrug in his voice. "Maybe that's because he saw that a better explanation wouldn't have been good for us. I don't know why. As a philosopher, I'm obviously curious. Humanly, I wish he had given us more information.

"But he knew Jesus was more than an explanation," he said firmly. "He's what we really need. If your friend is sick and dying, the most important thing he wants is not an explanation; he wants you to sit with him. He's terrified of being alone more than anything else. So God has not left us alone."

MAN OF SORROWS:
CHRIST WITH AIDS
—W. MAXWELL LAWTON

Painting commissioned for St. George's Cathedral, Cape Town by Archbishop Tutu of South Africa.

IF YOU WERE TO CALL EACH
ONE OF THE WITNESSES TO
JESUS' POST-RESURRECTION
APPEARANCES TO A COURT
OF LAW TO BE CROSS-EXAMINED
FOR JUST FIFTEEN MINUTES
EACH, AND YOU WENT AROUND
THE CLOCK WITHOUT A BREAK,
IT WOULD TAKE YOU FROM
BREAKFAST ON MONDAY UNTIL
DINNER ON FRIDAY TO HEAR
THEM ALL. A TOTAL OF 129
STRAIGHT HOURS OF
EYEWITNESS TESTIMONY.

If I find in myself a desire which no experience in this world can satisfy, the most probable explanation is that I was made for another world.—C.S. LEWIS

You're here because you know something. What you know you can't explain. But you feel it. You've felt it your entire life. That there's something wrong with the world. You don't know what it is but it's there, like a splinter in your mind driving you mad. It is this feeling that has brought you to me. Do you know what I'm talking about?

—Morpheus in *The Matrix*

I believe. Help me

Some people think that faith means a lack of doubt, but that's not true. One of my favorite Bible texts is about the man who comes to Jesus with his demon-possessed son, hoping that the boy would get healed. Jesus says all things are possible to those who believe. And the man's response is so powerful. He says, "I believe, but would you help me with my unbelief?"— *LYNN ANDERSON*

with my **un**belief!

+ + + "Forgive me for being blunt," I said in prefacing my question, "but ISN'T IT GROSSLY ARROGANT FOR CHRISTIANS TO CLAIM JESUS IS THE ONE AND ONLY WAY TO GOD? Why do Christians think they're justified in asserting that they're right and that everybody else in

the world is wrong?" + + + + + + + + + + + + + + +
+ + + "First," Ravi Zacharias said, "it's important to understand that
Christianity is not the only religion that claims exclusivity. For instance,
Muslims radically claim exclusivity. + + + + + + + + +

+ + + "As for Buddhism, it was born when Gautama Buddha rejected two fundamental assertions of Hinduism—the ultimate authority of the Vedas, which are their scriptures, and the caste system. Hinduism itself is absolutely uncompromising on two or three issues: the law of karma, which is the law of moral cause and effect, so that every birth is a rebirth that makes recompense for the previous life; the authority of the Vedas; and reincarnation." + + + + + I interrupted. "But I've heard Hindus say quite nobly that Hinduism is a very tolerant faith." + + + + + + + + + + + +

+ + + He smiled. "Whenever you hear that statement, don't take it at face value," he said. "What it really means is that Hinduism allows you to practice your religion so long as it buys into their notion of truth, which is syncretistic," he said. Syncretism is the attempt to blend together different

or even opposing beliefs. + + + + + + + + + + + + + + +
+ + + "As for Sikhism," he continued, "it came as a challenge to both
Hinduism and Buddhism. Then there are the atheists—they reject the
viewpoints of those who believe in God. And even Baha'ism, which claims

to be a cosmic embrace of all religions. ends up excluding the exclusivists! Therefore, the statement that Christians are arrogant by claiming exclusivity ignores the reality that every other major religion does as well." + + + + + "You believe that all truth—" I began. + + + + + + + +

"Is, by definition, exclusive," he said. "Yes, yes, I do. Truth excludes its opposite. Islam, Buddhism, Hinduism, and Christianity are not saying the same thing. They are distinct and mutually exclusive religious doctrines. THEY ALL CANNOT BE TRUE AT THE SAME TIME." - - -

GOD, IS THE HOLY BIBLE

OR IS THE KORAN HOLY?

BOTH, MAYBE?

54-61 98 88 90 92 100 116

REALLY HOLY?

The struggle with God is not lack of faith. It is faith. —*André Resner*

THERE ARE LOTS OF DIFFERENT KINDS OF DOUBTERS, Lynn Anderson told me. Some are rebellious, even though they may not identify themselves that way. They have the attitude, "I'm not going to let somebody run my life or do my thinking." Sometimes, a young person wants to rebel against his parents, and one way to do that is to rebel against the God they believe in.

Then there are people whose doubts stem from their disappointment with God. Like the girl I visited with yesterday. God says, "Seek and ask," but she's asked and he hasn't given. So she's wrestling with uncertainty. Was God serious? Was he even there?

Others have personal or family wounds. I talked a few weeks ago with a lady who underwent physical abuse from her mom and dad who were deeply religious—they'd make her kneel by the bed and pray and then beat her. I can see why she's got a problem with God! Others have been personally hurt in the sense of being rejected by a mate or their business has gone south or their health has gone bad. They're wondering, "If there's a God, why does this stuff happen?"

Then there are the intellectual doubts. This was where I was at. I was doing my best to intellectually undergird my faith, but there were people a lot smarter than me who didn't believe in God. I started to think, "Is faith only for the brilliant? How can faith be so important to God, and yet you've got to have an IQ of 197 to hang onto it?"

Seasons of life can make a big difference. Sometimes people are great believers while in college, but when they're young parents with their second baby and they're working sixty hours a week and the boss is on their back—they simply don't have time to reflect. And I don't think faith can develop without some contemplative time. If they don't make room for that, their faith is not going to grow and doubts will creep in.

WHY ARE PEOPLE PUNISHED INFINITELY FOR FINITE CRIMES?

What is the most heinous thing a person can do in this life? Most people, because they don't think much about God, will say it's harming animals or destroying the environment or hurting another person. And, no question, all of those are horrible. But they pale in light of the worst thing a person can do, which is to mock and dishonor and refuse to love the person that we owe absolutely everything to, which is our Creator, God himself. You have to understand that God is infinitely greater in his goodness, holiness, kindness, and justice than anyone else. To think that a person could go through their whole life constantly ignoring him, constantly mocking him by the way they choose to live without him, saying, "I couldn't care less about what you put me here to do. I couldn't care less about your values or your Son's death for me. I'm going to ignore all of that"—that's the ultimate sin. And the only punishment worthy of that is the ultimate punishment, which is everlasting separation from God. In the United States, the most serious crime—murder—is punishable by its most severe sanction, which is being separated from society for life in prison.

WHY DOESN'T GOD FORCE EVERYONE TO GO TO HEAVEN?

IF

God has given people free will
then there's no guarantee that everybody's
going to choose to cooperate with him. The option of
forcing everyone to go to heaven is immoral, because it's
dehumanizing; it strips them of the dignity of making their own
decision; it denies them their freedom of choice; and it treats them
as a means to an end. God can't make people's character for them, and
people who do evil or cultivate false beliefs start a slide away from God that
ultimately ends in hell. God respects human freedom. In fact, it would be
unloving—a sort of divine rape—to force people to accept heaven and God
if they didn't really want them. When God allows people to say "no" to
him, he actually respects and dignifies them. God doesn't like it, but
he quarantines them. This honors their freedom of choice.
He just will not override that. In fact, God considers people
so intrinsically valuable that he sent his Son, Jesus
Christ, to suffer and die so that they can, if they
choose, spend eternity in heaven
with him.

If there is no God, then morality is just a matter of personal taste, akin to statements like, 'Broccoli tastes good.' Well, it tastes good to some people but bad to others. There isn't any objective truth about that; it's a subjective matter of taste. And to say that killing innocent children is wrong would just be an expression of taste, saying, 'I don't like the killing of innocent children.'

"Like atheist Bertrand Russell, I don't see any reason to think that in the absence of God, the morality evolved by *homo sapiens* is objective. *AFTER ALL, IF THERE IS NO GOD, THEN WHAT'S SO SPECIAL ABOUT HUMAN BEINGS?* They're just accidental byproducts of nature

Curious roosters approach a fence at Sunnyside Farm in Rappahannock County, Va. The organically raised poultry is part of the farm's operation. (AP Photo/Richmond Times-Dispatch, Bruce Parker)

that have only recently evolved on a tiny speck of dust lost somewhere in a mindless universe and are doomed to perish forever in a relatively short time.

"But, we all know deep down that, in fact, objective moral values do exist. All we have to do to see that is to simply ask ourselves: 'Is torturing a child for fun really a morally neutral act?' I'm persuaded you'd say, 'No, that's not morally neutral; it's really wrong to do that.' And you'll say that in full cognizance of the Darwinian theory of evolution and all the rest".

Pasa Balter, fourth from left, stands among a group of children wearing concentration camp uniforms behind barbed wire fencing as they were liberated from the Nazi concentration camp at Auschwitz, Poland, by Russian soldiers in April, 1945. Balter bears the heartbreak of having lost most of her family. (AP Photo/ho)

The Holy Bible for Prosecution Exhibit Only

EVIDENCE

Case No. _____

Evidence Description

_____

_____

Place Evidence Found

HOLY BIBLE

"Faith is a rational response to the evidence of God's self-revelation in ... the Scriptures and his resurrected Son."
—*W. Bingham Hunters*

We like to focus on the upbeat Psalms, but sixty percent of them are laments, with people screaming out,

"GOD, WHERE ARE YOU?"

Why, O LORD, do you stand far off?
Why do you hide yourself in times of trouble?
Psalm 10:1

GOD, WHERE ARE YOU?

"GOD, WHERE ARE YOU?"

Normal faith is allowed to beat on God's chest and complain.

GOD,
I HAVE A FRIEND WHO
IS HINDU.
HE'S A REALLY NICE GUY—
EVERYBODY LIKES HIM.

ARE YOU GOING TO SEND
HIM TO HELL
WHEN HE DIES?

He is not far from any one of us. —ACTS 17:27

He is not far from any one of us. —ACTS 17:27

Two victims of the fire in Ycua Bolanos supermarket are carried out of the building in Asuncion, Paraguay on Sunday, August 1, 2004. The fire

He is not far from any one of us. –ACTS 17:27

He is not far from any one of us. —ACTS 17:27

He is not far from any one of us. —ACTS 17:27

83

1Now *faith* is being sure of what we hope for and certain of what we do not see. 2This is what the ancients were commended for.

3By *faith* we understand that the universe was formed at God's command, so that what is seen was not made out of what was visible.

4By *faith* Abel offered God a better sacrifice than Cain did. By *faith* he was commended as a righteous man, when God spoke well of his offerings. And by *faith* he still speaks, even though he is dead.

5By *faith* Enoch was taken from this life, so that he did not experience death; he could not be found, because God had taken him away. For before he was taken, he was commended as one who pleased God. 6And without *faith* it is impossible to please God, because anyone who comes to him must believe that he exists and that he rewards those who earnestly seek him.

7By *faith* Noah, when warned about things not yet seen, in holy fear built an ark to save his family. By his *faith* he condemned the world and became heir of the righteousness that comes by *faith*.

8By *faith* Abraham, when called to go to a place he would later receive as his inheritance, obeyed and went, even though he did not know where he was going. 9By *faith* he made his home in the promised land like a stranger in a foreign country; he lived in tents, as did Isaac and Jacob, who were heirs with him of the same promise. 10For he was looking forward to the city with foundations, whose architect and builder is God.

11By *faith* Abraham, even though he was past age--and Sarah herself was barren--was enabled to become a father because he considered him *faith*ful who had made the promise. 12And so from this one man, and he as good as dead, came descendants as numerous as the stars in the sky and as countless as the sand on the seashore.

13All these people were still living by *faith* when they died. They did not receive the things promised; they only saw them and welcomed them from a distance. And they admitted that they were aliens and strangers on earth. 14People who say such things show that they are looking for a country of their own. 15If they had been thinking of the country they had left, they would have had opportunity to return. 16Instead, they were longing for a better country--a heavenly one. Therefore God is not ashamed to be called their God, for he has prepared a city for them.

17By *faith* Abraham, when God tested him, offered Isaac as a sacrifice. He who had received the promises was about to sacrifice his one and only son, 18even though God had said to him, "It is through Isaac that your offspring will be reckoned." 19Abraham reasoned that God could raise the dead, and figuratively speaking, he did receive Isaac back from death.

20By *faith* Isaac blessed Jacob and Esau in regard to their future.

21By *faith* Jacob, when he was dying, blessed each of Joseph's sons, and worshiped as he leaned on the top of his staff.

22By *faith* Joseph, when his end was near, spoke about the exodus of the Israelites from Egypt and gave instructions about his bones.

23By *faith* Moses' parents hid him for three months after he was born, because they saw he was no ordinary child, and they were not afraid of the king's edict.

24By *faith* Moses, when he had grown up, refused to be known as the son of Pharaoh's daughter. 25He chose to be mistreated along with the people of God rather than to enjoy the pleasures of sin for a short time. 26He regarded disgrace for the sake of Christ as of greater value than the treasures of Egypt, because he was looking ahead to his reward. 27By *faith* he left Egypt, not fearing the king's anger; he persevered because he saw him who is invisible. 28By *faith* he kept the Passover and the sprinkling of blood, so that the destroyer of the firstborn would not touch the firstborn of Israel.

29By *faith* the people passed through the Red Sea as on dry land; but when the Egyptians tried to do so, they were drowned. 30By *faith* the walls of Jericho fell, after the people had marched around them for seven days.

31By *faith* the prostitute Rahab, because she welcomed the spies, was not killed with those who were disobedient.

32And what more shall I say? I do not have time to tell about Gideon, Barak, Samson, Jephthah, David, Samuel and the prophets, 33who through *faith* conquered kingdoms, administered justice, and gained what was promised; who shut the mouths of lions, 34quenched the fury of the flames, and escaped the edge of the sword; whose weakness was turned to strength; and who became powerful in battle and routed foreign armies. 35Women received back their dead, raised to life again. Others were tortured and refused to be released, so that they might gain a better resurrection. 36Some faced jeers and flogging, while still others were chained and put in prison. 37They were stoned; they were sawed in two; they were put to death by the sword. They went about in sheepskins and goatskins, destitute, persecuted and mistreated-- 38**the world was not worthy of them.** They wandered in deserts and mountains, and in caves and holes in the ground.

39These were all commended for their *faith*, yet none of them received what had been promised. 40God had planned something better for us so that only together with us would they be made perfect.

† † † † † † † † † † †

Bystanders protect themselves seconds after a second explosion (left) detonated outside of the Atlanta Northside Family Planning Services building in Atlanta on Thursday, Jan. 16, 1997. Two explosions rocked the building containing an abortion clinic. (AP Photo/Alan Mothner)

The Bible makes it clear that because of our sinful nature, we continue to do things as Christians that we shouldn't. We're not perfect in this world. And unfortunately, some of the evil deeds THE CRUSADES, THE INQUISITION, THE SALEM WITCH TRIALS, EXPLORATION BY MISSIONARIES, committed through history may have, indeed, been committed by Christians. When that has happened, they've acted contrary to the teachings of Jesus.

IAN WILSON [*British author*] discusses the possibility that

JESUS MAY HAVE BEEN A MASTER HYPNOTIST,

which could explain the supposedly supernatural aspects of his life.

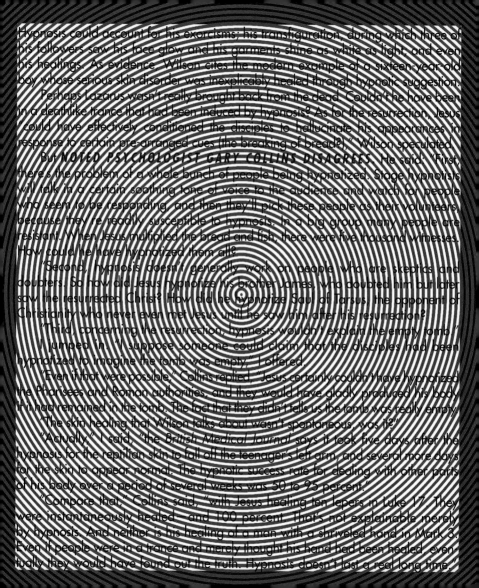

Hypnosis could account for his exorcisms, his transfiguration, during which three of his followers saw his face glow and his garments shine as white as light, and even his healings. As evidence, Wilson cites the modern example of a sixteen-year-old boy whose serious skin disorder was inexplicably healed through hypnotic suggestion.

Perhaps Lazarus wasn't really brought back from the dead. Couldn't he have been in a deathlike trance that had been induced by hypnosis? As for the resurrection, Jesus could have effectively conditioned the disciples to hallucinate his appearances in response to certain pre-arranged cues (the breaking of bread?)," Wilson speculated.

But *NOTED PSYCHOLOGIST GARY COLLINS DISAGREES.* He said: "First, there's the problem of a whole bunch of people being hypnotized. Stage hypnotists will talk in a certain soothing tone of voice to the audience and watch for people who seem to be responding, and then they'll pick these people as their volunteers, because they're readily susceptible to hypnosis. In a big group many people are resistant. When Jesus multiplied the bread and fish, there were five thousand witnesses. How could he have hypnotized them all?

"Second, hypnosis doesn't generally work on people who are skeptics and doubters. So how did Jesus hypnotize his brother James, who doubted him but later saw the resurrected Christ? How did he hypnotize Saul of Tarsus, the opponent of Christianity who never even met Jesus until he saw him after his resurrection?

"Third, concerning the resurrection, hypnosis wouldn't explain the empty tomb."

I jumped in. "I suppose someone could claim that the disciples had been hypnotized to imagine the tomb was empty," I offered.

"Even if that were possible," Collins replied, "Jesus certainly couldn't have hypnotized the Pharisees and Roman authorities, and they would have gladly produced his body if it had remained in the tomb. The fact that they didn't tells us the tomb was really empty."

"The skin healing that Wilson talks about wasn't spontaneous, was it?"

"Actually," I said, "the *British Medical Journal* says it took five days after the hypnosis for the reptilian skin to fall off the teenager's left arm, and several more days for the skin to appear normal. The hypnotic success rate for dealing with other parts of his body over a period of several weeks was 50 to 95 percent."

"Compare that," Collins said, "with Jesus healing ten lepers in Luke 17. They were instantaneously healed — and 100 percent. That's not explainable merely by hypnosis. And neither is his healing of a man with a shriveled hand in Mark 3. Even if people were in a trance and merely thought his hand had been healed, eventually they would have found out the truth. Hypnosis doesn't last a real long time

"Yes,
[the apostles] were
willing to die for their beliefs. But,"
I added, "so have Muslims and Mormons and followers
of Jim Jones and David Koresh. This may show that
they were fanatical, but let's face it: it doesn't
prove that what they believed is true."

"Wait a minute—think carefully about the
difference," Moreland insisted. "Muslims
might be willing to die for their belief
that Allah revealed himself to
Muhammad, but this revelation
was not done in a publicly
observable way. So they
could be wrong about
it. They may
sincerely think
it's true, but
they can't
know
for
a

fact,
because
they didn't
witness it them-
selves.

"However, the apostles
were willing to die for something
they had seen with their own eyes and
touched with their own hands. They were
in a unique position not to just believe Jesus
rose from the dead but to know for sure. And when
you've got eleven credible people with no ulterior
motives, with nothing to gain and a lot to lose, who all agree
they observed something with their own eyes—now
you've got some difficulty explaining
that away."

THOMAS.

St. Thomas.

St Thomas his Martyrdom.

DEATHS OF THE TWELVE APOSTLES

1. Andrew—crucified
2. Bartholomew—beaten then crucified
3. James, son of Alphaeus—stoned to death
4. James, son of Zebedee—beheaded
5. John—exiled for his faith; died of old age
6. Judas [not Iscariot]—stoned to death
7. Matthew—speared to death
8. Peter—crucified upside down
9. Philip—crucified
10. Simon—crucified
11. Thomas—speared to death
12. Matthias—stoned to death

...d of an Indian King he was thrust...

John xi. Thomas which is called Didimus said unto his fellow-disciples, Let us also goe, that we may die...

At the time of Jesus, the Jews had been persecuted for 700 years. Many Jews had been scattered and lived as captives in other nations.

However, we still see Jews today, while we don't see Hittites, Perizzites, Persians, Babylonians, and other people who had been living in that time. Why? Because these people got captured by other nations, intermarried, and lost their national identity. Why didn't that happen to the Jews? Because the things that made the Jews, Jews–the social structures that gave them their national identity–were unbelievably important to them. The Jews would pass these structures down to their children, celebrate them in synagogue meetings every Sabbath, and reinforce them with their rituals, because they knew if they didn't, there soon would be no Jews left. They would be assimilated into the cultures that captured them.

BC

000   800   600   400   200   BC

And there's another reason why these social institutions were so important: they believed these institutions were entrusted to them by God. They believed that to abandon these institutions would be to risk their souls being damned to hell after death.

Now a rabbi named Jesus appears from a lower-class region. He teaches for three years, gathers a following of lower- and middle-class people, gets in trouble with the authorities, and gets crucified along with thirty thousand other Jewish men who are executed during this time period.

But five weeks after he's crucified, over ten thousand Jews are following him and claiming that he is the initiator of a new religion. And get this: they're willing to give up or alter all five of the social institutions that they have been taught since childhood have such importance both sociologically and theologically. Something very big was going on!

GOD, WERE THE CRUSADES

REALLY YOUR IDEA?

41 86 122

I have spoken
in many Islamic countries,
where it's tough to talk about Jesus. Virtually

every Muslim who has come to follow Christ

has done so, first, because of the love

of Christ expressed through a Christian,

or second, because of a vision, a dream,

or some other supernatural intervention.

_____ has a more intricate doctrine

_____ Islam, and I think it's

_____ raordinary that God uses

that sensitivity to the supernatural world in which he speaks in visions and dreams and reveals himself. One of India's greatest converts was a Sikh, Sundar Singh, who came to know Christ through an appearance of Christ in his room in a dream one night. It had a tremendous impact on his life and he became a Christian. This reveals that God can undertake beyond our own

Uchisar, a fortress-like town carved into a prominent peak of about 4,300 feet, towers above the central Turkish region of Cappadocia, Oct. 1999. The ancient Hittites and early Byzantine Christians dug homes out of the soft volcanic stone known as tuff. *(AP Photo/John Biemer)*

Jewish ossuary with the name 'Caiphus', in Hebrew, carved on its side. Caiaphas was the high priest in Jerusalem at the time of Jesus' trial. The ossuary was found in a Jewish burial in Jerusalem.

Norman L. Geisler started his discussion of the archaeological evidence by quoting the words of Jesus, who said: "I have spoken to you of earthly things and you do not believe; how then will you believe if I speak of heavenly things?"

"Conversely," said Geisler, "if we can trust the Bible when it's telling us about straightforward earthly things that can be verified, then we can trust it in areas where we can't directly verify it in an empirical way."

"How, then, has the Bible been corroborated?" I asked.

"There have been thousands—not hundreds—of archaeological finds in the Middle East that support the picture presented in the biblical record. There was a discovery not long ago confirming King David. The patriarchs—the narratives about Abraham, Isaac, and Jacob—were once considered legendary, but as more has become known these stories are increasingly corroborated. The destruction of Sodom and Gomorrah was thought to be mythological until evidence was uncovered that all five of the cities mentioned in Genesis were, in fact, situated just as the Old Testament said. As far as their destruction goes, archaeologist Clifford Wilson said there is 'permanent evidence of the great conflagration that took place in the long distant past.'

"As the great archaeologist William F. Albright declared, 'There can be no doubt that archaeology has confirmed the substantial historicity of the Old Testament tradition.'"

Two men stand on the foundations of the ancient Khirbet Qumran ruins which lie on the northwestern shore of the Dead Sea in Jordan, Jan. 14, 1957. The ruins are above the caves in which the Dead Sea Scrolls were discovered in 1947. In the background are the Hills of Moab with the Dead Sea below. *(AP Photo)*

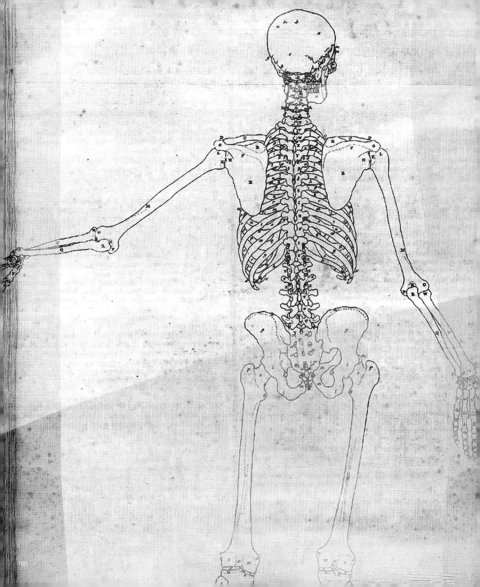

Let's pretend we didn't have any of the New Testament or other Christian writings.

What would we be able to conclude about Jesus from ancient non-Christian sources, such as Josephus, the Talmud, Tacitus, Pliny the Younger, and others?

We would still have a considerable amount of important historical evidence; in fact, it would provide a kind of outline for the life of Jesus. We would know that

1. Jesus was a Jewish teacher;

2. Many people believed that he performed healings and exorcisms;

3. Some people believed he was the Messiah;

4. He was rejected by the Jewish leaders;

5. He was crucified under Pontius Pilate in the reign of Tiberius;

6. Despite this shameful death, his followers, who believed that he was still alive, spread beyond Palestine so that there were multitudes of them in Rome by A.D. 64; and

7. All kinds of people from the cities and countryside—men and women, slave and free—worshiped him as God.

The danger of a Western perspective is thinking that if something isn't neatly packaged, it's no good. And unfortunately, some Western Christians think that unless a person says the creed just like they do, they don't know God.

Yet what does an infant know of his mother? He knows she nourishes him, she changes him, she embraces him, she kisses him—she must be a friend. That child doesn't know his mother as well as he will when he's eighteen. But he knows her enough to love her. I believe that as God reveals himself there are levels of understanding that are bound to vary.

(((In the movie *Contact*, scientists are scanning the skies for signs of intelligent life in space. Their radiotelescopes just receive static–random sounds. It's reasonable to assume there's no intelligence behind that. Then one day they begin receiving a transmission of prime numbers, which are numbers divisible only by themselves and one. The scientists reason that it's too improbable that there would be a natural cause behind a string of numbers like that.)))
(((This wasn't merely unorganized static; it was information, a message with content. From that, they concluded there was an

intelligent cause behind it. Carl Sagan himself once said, "the receipt of a single message from space" would be enough to know there's an intelligence out there.)))   (((That's reasoning by analogy–we know that where there's intelligent communication, there's an intelligent cause.)))   (((Each cell in the human body contains more information than in all thirty volumes of the *Encyclopaedia Britannica*. It's certainly reasonable to make the inference that this isn't the random product of unguided nature, but it's the unmistakable sign of an Intelligent Designer.)))   (((

He is not far from any one of us. —ACTS 17:27

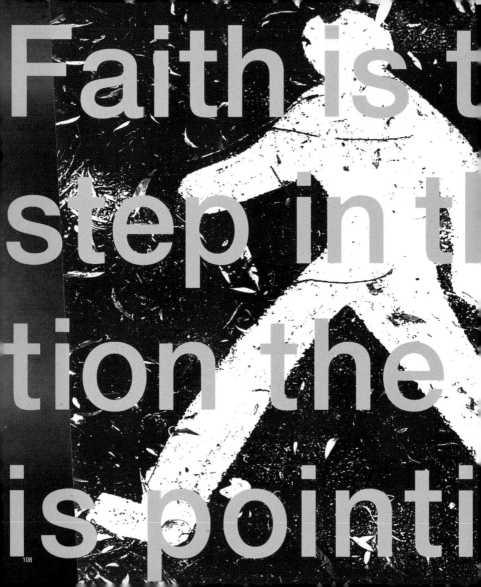

Faith is t
step in tl
tion the
is pointi

aking a
ne direc-
evidence
ng.

light f... ...ho... ...ose who don't...

"…Now I'll give you something to believe. I'm just one hundred and one, five months and a day."

"I ca'n't believe that!" said Alice.

"Ca'n't you?" the Queen said in a pitying tone. "Try again: draw a long breath, and shut your eyes."

Alice laughed. "There's no use trying," she said: "one ca'n't believe impossible things."

"I daresay you haven't had much practice," said the Queen. "When I was your age, I always did it for half-an-hour a day. Why, sometimes I've believed as many as six impossible things before breakfast…"

—LEWIS CARROLL
Through the Looking Glass and What Alice Found There

You can have very little faith in thick ice and it will hold you up just fine; you can have enormous faith in thin ice and you can drown. It's not the amount of faith you can muster that matters up front. It may be tiny, like a mustard seed. But your faith must be invested in something solid.

"What's he [Nick] say?" Abagail asked.
"He says…"
Ralph cleared his throat; the feather
stuck in the band of his hat jiggled.
"He says that he don't believe in God."
The message relayed,
he looked unhappily down at his shoes
and waited for the explosion.
But she only chuckled, got up, and
walked across to Nick. She took one of
his hands and patted it.
"Bless you, Nick, but that don't matter.
He believes in *you*."
—Stephen King, *The Stand*

But God demonstrates
his own love for us
in this: While we were
still sinners,
Christ died for us.
—Romans 5:8

The Rich Man and Lazarus (LUKE 16:19-31)

"There was a rich man who was dressed in purple and fine linen and lived in luxury every day. At his gate was laid a beggar named Lazarus, covered with sores and longing to eat what fell from the rich man's table. Even the dogs came and licked his sores.

"The time came when the beggar died and the angels carried him to Abraham's side. The rich man also died and was buried. In hell, where he was in torment, he looked up and saw Abraham far away, with Lazarus by his side. So he called to him, 'Father Abraham, have pity on me and send Lazarus to dip the tip of his finger in water and cool my tongue, because I am in agony in this fire.'

"But Abraham replied, 'Son, remember that in your lifetime you received your good things, while Lazarus received bad things, but now he is comforted here and you are in agony. And besides all this, between us and you a great chasm has been fixed, so that those who want to go from here to you cannot, nor can anyone cross over from there to us.'

"He answered, 'Then I beg you, father, send Lazarus to my father's house, for I have five brothers. Let him warn them, so that they will not also come to this place of torment.'

"Abraham replied, 'They have Moses and the Prophets; let them listen to them.'

" 'No, father Abraham,' he said, 'but if someone from the dead goes to them, they will repent.'

"He said to him, 'If they do not listen to Moses and the Prophets, they will not be convinced even if someone rises from the dead.' "

On my door there's a cartoon
of two turtles. One says,
"Sometimes I'd like to ask why he
allows poverty, famine, and
injustice when he could do
something about it."
The other turtle says,
"I'm afraid God might ask me the
same question."
Those who have Jesus' heart
toward hurting people need to
live out their faith by alleviating
suffering where they can,
by making a difference,
by embodying
his love in practical ways.
—Peter John Kreeft

Lynn Anderson laid the Bible back on the table and then scanned the room in search of an impromptu illustration. Apparently unable to find a suitable prop, he reached into his pocket and withdrew his hand. "Okay," he said, "I'm holding something. Do you know what it is?"

I ventured a guess: "A coin."

"But you don't know for sure," he said. "That's your opinion. Our faith is not our opinion. Let me tell you I've got a quarter in my hand. Do you believe that?"

"Sure," I said.

"I'm telling you it's true, but you haven't seen it. That's faith. Hebrews says faith is the evidence of things not seen." Anderson smiled. "Watch as I completely destroy your faith." With that, he opened his hand to reveal a quarter. "Now it's no longer faith; it's knowledge."

He tossed the quarter on the table.

"Sometimes people think that faith is knowing something is true beyond any doubt whatsoever, and so they try to prove faith through empirical evidence," he said. "But that's the wrong approach."

He gestured toward the coin. "You can see and touch that quarter, so you don't need faith. God, for his own reasons, has not subjected himself to that kind of proof."

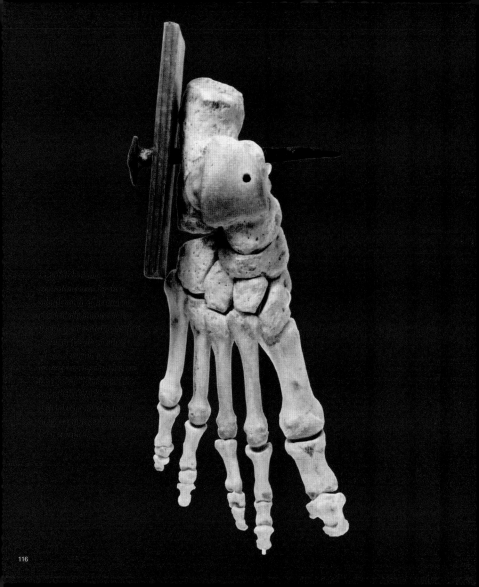

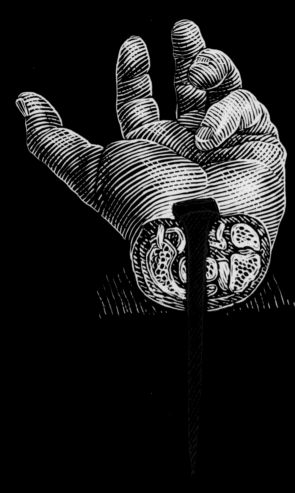

BY ANALYZING the medical and historical data, Dr. Alexander Metherell, a physician who also holds a doctorate in engineering, concluded Jesus could not have survived the gruesome rigors of crucifixion, much less the gaping wound that pierced his lung and heart. In fact, even before the crucifixion he was in serious to critical condition and suffering from hypovolemic shock as the result of a horrific flogging. The idea that he somehow swooned on the cross and **pretended to be dead** lacks any evidential basis. Roman executioners were grimly efficient, knowing that they themselves would face death if any of their victims were to come down from the cross alive. Even if Jesus had somehow lived through the torture, his ghastly condition could never have inspired a worldwide movement based on the premise that he had gloriously triumphed over the grave.

☐ A.   LUNATIC

☐ B.   Son of God

☐ C.   devil of hell

I am trying here to prevent anyone saying the really foolish thing that people often say about Him: "I'm ready to accept Jesus as a great moral teacher, but I don't accept His claim to be God." That is the one thing we must not say. A man who was merely a man and said the sort of things Jesus said would not be a great moral teacher. He would either be a lunatic ... or else he would be the Devil of Hell. You must make your choice. Either this man was, and is, the Son of God: or else a madman or something worse. You can shut Him up for a fool, you can spit at Him and kill Him as a demon; or you can fall at His feet and call Him Lord and God. But let us not come with any patronizing nonsense about His being a great human teacher. He has not left that open to us. He did not intend to. —C S L E W I S

Those who believe they believe in God
but without passion in the heart,
without anguish of mind,
without uncertainty,
without doubt,
and even at times without despair,
believe only in the idea of God,
and not in God himself.

—Madeleine L'Engle

IF FAITH NEVER ENCOUNTERS DOUBT, IF TRUTH NEVER
STRUGGLES WITH ERROR, IF GOOD NEVER BATTLES
WITH EVIL,   HOW CAN FAITH KNOW ITS OWN POWER?
IN MY OWN PILGRIMAGE, IF I HAVE TO CHOOSE BETWEEN
A FAITH THAT HAS STARED DOUBT IN THE EYE
AND MADE IT BLINK,
OR A NAIVE FAITH THAT HAS NEVER KNOWN THE FIRING
LINE OF DOUBT, I WILL CHOOSE
THE FORMER EVERY TIME.

JESUS CHRIST DIDN'T COME INTO THIS WORLD TO MAKE DEAD PEOPLE LIVE. HE CAME SO THAT

WORLD TO MAKE BAD PEOPLE GOOD. HE CAME INTO THIS
THOSE WHO ARE DEAD TO GOD CAN COME ALIVE TO GOD.

The truth will set you free.—JESUS

THE MISSING LINK IS STILL MIS

DARWIN CONCEDED that the lack of fossil evidence for the transitions between various species of animals "is perhaps the most obvious and serious objection" to his theory, although he confidently predicted that future discoveries would vindicate him.

Fast forward to 1979. David M. Raup, the curator of the Field Museum of Natural History in Chicago, said:

> We are now about one hundred and twenty years after Darwin and the knowledge of the fossil record has been greatly expanded. We now have a quarter of a million fossil species, but the situation hasn't changed much.... We have even fewer examples of evolutionary transition than we had in Darwin's time.

What the fossil record does show is that in rocks dated back some five hundred and seventy million years, there is the sudden appearance of nearly all the animal phyla, and they appear fully formed, "without a trace of the evolutionary ancestors that Darwinists require." It's a phemonenon that points more readily toward a Creator than Darwinism.

SING

GOD, IF YOU DO MIRACLES ARE YOU TOO BUSY DOING

WHY ARE THEY SO RARE?

OTHER THINGS?

EVIDENCE

Warning!!
Police Seal

DO NOT
REMOVE

"Faith is a rational response to the evidence of God's self-revelation in nature..." —*W. Bingham Hunters*

they wanna ██████ ████ ████ ████ closet case nom...

Jim: What about Preacher Hilton?

Dave: I don't get along with him religiously. My views on religion change day to day. I have a lot of respect for him 'cause he'll help people. Dude's given me his last dollar. He's fed me when he even didn't have something to eat himself. He doesn't look at us like we're any different from him. He looks at us like we're people.

Jim: What about youth service programs?

Dave: Most of the programs, I think, are basically trying but they ain't doing ███. Dude, there's fifty beds for a thousand kids.

Jim: What about all the rules?

Dave: The rules suck, man. People shouldn't be concerned with what color my hair is or what length it is or what my t-shirt says. They should care about if this kid is hungry or not. Does this kid need a bath? Does this kid need a place to sleep?

Jim: Why don't programs work?

Dave: Because, dude, they come down too hard. The rules are too extreme, man. I mean, they say they've gotta change the street kids' lives. Well, that's true. But you can't take somebody from point A to point Z overnight. You can't make me a ███ suburban teenager now, after what's gone down. It'll never happen. My whole attitude, my whole bearing, is ███ different than the attitude of people in the suburbs.

Jim: Why do you think that is?

Dave: 'Cause of what I've had to do to survive. When you've had to ███ and eat out of dumpsters, it's a little different than if you could just walk up and say, "I'm hungry, mom." It's hard to follow a law when you've gotta eat. You're gonna dumpster-dive. You're gonna panhandle. You're gonna sell your body. It's hard to follow a program when you don't believe in anything. It's hard to believe in God if you don't believe in anything. There's my answer. See, all these things I'm supposed to believe in — God, the police, the programs — I don't believe in them. ███, man, what I really believe is that I'm gonna walk and go buy a book 'cause I got three dollars in my pocket. We are the black sheep of the American family. Quit looking for an answer, Jim. There ███ ain't one. ███ yeah, I'm still looking for God's telephone number.

SEVERAL YEARS EARLIER, Marc had been shoveling snow on his driveway when his wife said she was going to move the car and asked him to watch their young daughter. As the car backed out, they were suddenly thrust into the worst nightmare that parents can imagine: their toddler was crushed beneath a wheel.

So deep was Marc's initial despair that he had to ask God to help him breathe, to help him eat, to help him function at the most fundamental level. Otherwise, he was paralyzed by the emotional pain. But he increasingly felt God's presence, his grace, his warmth, his comfort, and very slowly, over time, his wounds began to heal.

Having experienced God at his point of greatest need, Marc would emerge from this crucible a changed person, abandoning his career in business to attend seminary. Through his suffering—though he never would have chosen it, though it was horribly painful, though it was life-shattering at the time—Marc has been transformed into someone who would devote the rest of life to bringing God's compassion to others who are alone in their desperation.

In the pulpit for the first time, Marc was able to draw on his own experiences with God in the depths of sorrow. People were captivated because his own loss had given him special insights, empathy, and credibility. In the end, dozens of them responded by saying they too wanted to know this Jesus, this **GOD OF TEARS**. Now other hearts were being healed because of Marc's having been broken. From one couple's despair emerges new hope for many.

"Sometimes skeptics scoff at the Bible saying that God can cause good to emerge from our pain if we run toward him instead of away from him," Marc said. "But I've watched it happen in my own life. I've experienced God's goodness through deep pain, and no skeptic can dispute that. The God who the skeptic denies is the same God who held our hands in the deep, dark places, who strengthened our marriage, who deepened our faith, who increased our reliance on him, who gave us two more children, and who infused our lives with new purpose and meaning so that we can make a difference to others."

I asked gently, "Do you wish you had more answers about why suffering happens in the first place?"

"We live in a broken world; Jesus was honest enough to tell us we'd have trials and tribulations. Sure, I'd like to understand more about why. But the ultimate answer is Jesus' presence. That sounds sappy, I know. But just wait—when your world is rocked, you don't want philosophy or theology as much as you want the reality of Christ. He was the answer for me. He was the very answer we needed."

God, if he is all-wise, knows not only the present but the future. And he knows not only present good and evil but future good and evil. If his wisdom vastly exceeds ours, as the hunter's exceeds the bear's [See pages 38-39], it is at least possible that a loving God could deliberately tolerate horrible things like starvation because he foresees that in the long run that more people will be better and happier than if he miraculously intervened. You see, God has specifically shown us very clearly how this can work. He has demonstrated how the very worst thing that has ever happened in the history of the world ended up being the very best thing that has ever happened in the history of the world. I'm referring to dei-cide, the death of God himself on the cross. At the time, nobody saw how anything good could ever result from this tragedy. And yet God foresaw that the result would be the opening of heaven to human beings. So **the worst tragedy in history** brought about the most glorious event in history. And if it happened there—if the ultimate evil can result in the ultimate good—it can happen elsewhere, even in our own individual lives. Here, God lifts the curtain and let's us see it. Elsewhere he simply says, "Trust me."

See

"THERE'S ONE OTHER category of evidence you haven't asked about," philosopher J. P. Moreland remarked.

My mind reviewed our interview. "I give up," I said. "What is it?"

"It's the ongoing encounter with the resurrected Christ that happens all over the world, in every culture, to people from all kinds of backgrounds and personalities–well educated and not, rich and poor, thinkers and feelers, men and women," he said. "They all will testify that more than any single thing in their lives, Jesus Christ has changed them."

"I assume you've had an encounter like that," I said. "Tell me about it."

"In 1968 I was a cynical chemistry major at the University of Missouri, when I was

God

confronted with the fact that if I examined the claims of Jesus Christ critically but with an open mind, there was more than enough evidence for me to believe it.

"So I took a step of faith in the same direction the evidence was pointing, by receiving Jesus as my forgiver and leader, and I began to relate to him—to the resurrected Christ—in a very real and ongoing way.

"In three decades I've had hundreds of specific answers to prayers, I've had things happen that simply cannot be explained by natural explanations, and I have experienced a changed life beyond anything I could have imagined."

WHAT DO YOU

Once I was talking with an ex-Marine who said, "I'm miserable. I've got a wife and kids, and I'm making more money than I can spend with both hands, and I'm sleeping with every woman in town-and I hate myself. You've got to help me, but don't give me any of that God talk because I can't believe that stuff."

We talked for hours. Finally, I said, "Maybe you think you're shooting straight with me, but I'm not sure you are. I don't think your problem is that you can't believe; I think it's that you won't believe because you're afraid to give up the things that help get you through the night."

He thought for a while and then said, "Yeah, I guess that's true. I can't imagine sleeping with just one woman. I can't imagine going with less money than I make-which I'd have to do because I lie to get it." He was finally trying to be honest.

WANT ? (16442)

With that, Lynn Anderson's voice dropped to an intense whisper. "And here's my point," he said. "That man would argue and argue for hours about his cerebral doubts. He would convince people that he couldn't believe because he had too many intellectual objections. But they were just a smokescreen. They were merely a fog he used to obscure his real hesitations about God."

"Here's my experience," Anderson said in summary. "When you scratch below the surface, there's either a will to believe or there's a will not to believe. That's the core of it."

"So you're saying faith is a choice," I said. Anderson nodded in agreement. "That's exactly right," he replied. "It's a choice."

He is not far from any one of us. —ACTS 17:27

He is not far from any one of us. —ACTS 17:27

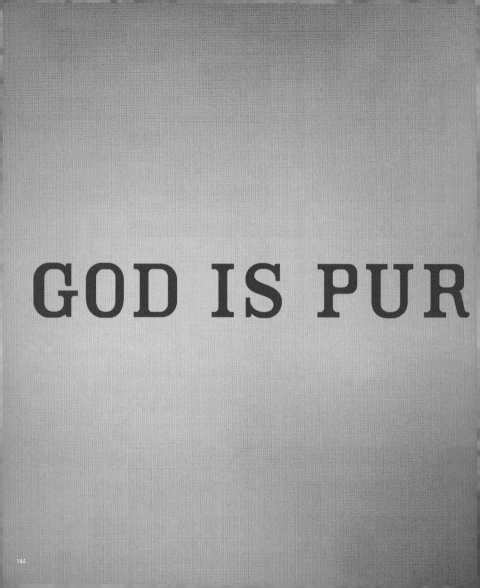

GOD IS PUR

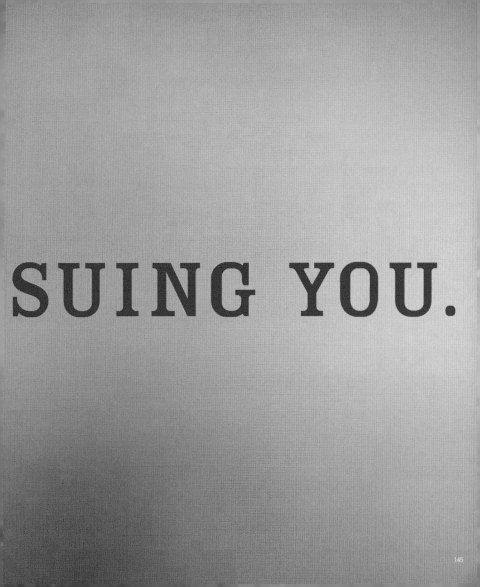

SUING YOU.

WHO DO YOU SAY I AM?

Text in this book was excerpted from the 1998 book *The Case for Christ* (CFC) and the 2000 book *The Case for Faith* (CFF) by Lee Strobel.

PLEASE USE THIS REFERENCE GUIDE TO LOCATE MORE IN-DEPTH DISCUSSIONS OF THESE CRITICAL TOPICS.

CREATIVE DEVELOPMENT
MARK ARNOLD, PETE GALL, KURT WILSON
With special thanks to Jon Arnold, JC Dillon and Nancy Duarte for valuable feedback throughout the creative process and to Connie Porte for project support.

ARTIST CREDITS

12	photographer:	Peter Hellebrand	
16-17	photographer:	Hans Balliet	yoki@alexandria.cc
22-23	photographer:	Nils Vik	www.nilsvik.com
46	artist:	W. Maxwell Lawton	www.maxwelllawton@yahoo.com
66	photographer:	Rene Cerney	www.freewebmastersresource.com
67	photographer:	Michal Zacharzewski	www.sxc.hu
68-69	photographer:	Nils Vik	www.nilsvik.com
78	photographer:	Bjrrn Brrresen	bjorn_NOSPAM@root.no
82	photographer:	Katje Zanetta Borba	katje79@yahoo.com.br
90	artist:	Caravaggio	www.artres.com
102	photographer:	Jyn Meyer	www.jynmeyer.com
103	photographer:	Paul Preacher	www.paulpreacher.com
117	artist:	Clint Hansen	www.scotthull.com
128	photographer:	Andy Anderson	www.andyandersonphoto.com
130	photographer:	Jim Goldberg	www.magnumphotos.com
136-137	photographer:	Nils Vik	www.nilsvik.com
142	photographer:	Brandon Bennight	

Images on pages 14, 15, 36, 70, 71, 79, 80-81, 83 and 86 from AP/Wide World Photos

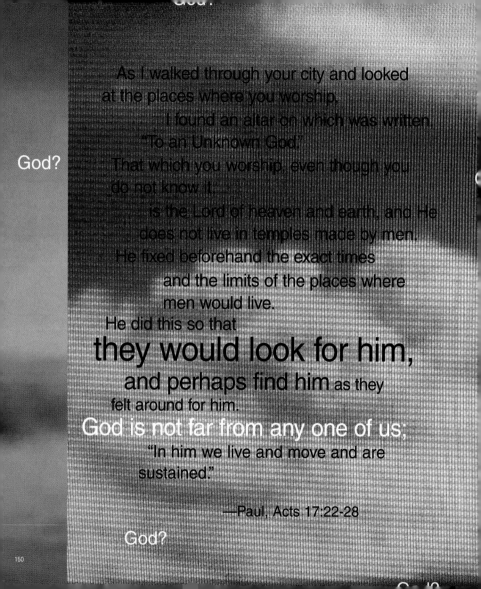

God?

As I walked through your city and looked
at the places where you worship,
    I found an altar on which was written,
    "To an Unknown God."
That which you worship, even though you
do not know it,
    is the Lord of heaven and earth, and He
    does not live in temples made by men.
He fixed beforehand the exact times
    and the limits of the places where
    men would live.
He did this so that

they would look for him,
and perhaps find him as they
felt around for him.
God is not far from any one of us;
    "In him we live and move and are
    sustained."

—Paul, Acts 17:22-28

God?

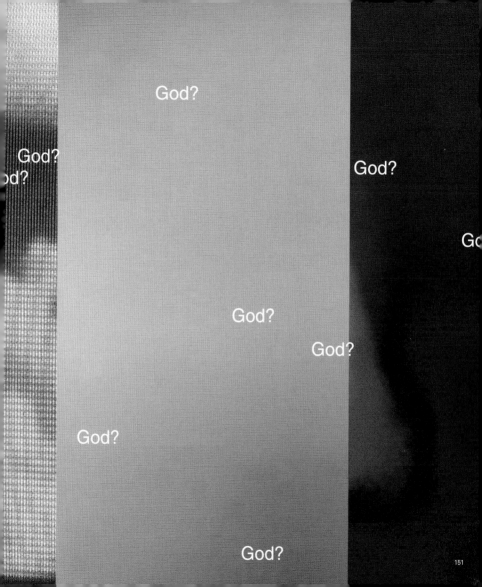

Only in a world where faith
is difficult can faith exist.

God?